A CENTURY *of*
LEEDS

View of Briggate looking north, *c*. 1900.

A CENTURY of LEEDS

BRETT HARRISON

SUTTON PUBLISHING

First published in the United Kingdom in 1999 by Sutton Publishing Limited
in association with the West Yorkshire Archive Service

This new paperback edition first published in 2007 by
Sutton Publishing, an imprint of NPI Media Group
Cirencester Road · Chalford · Stroud · Gloucestershire · GL6 8PE

British Library Cataloguing in Publication Data
A catalogue record for this book is available from the British Library.

ISBN 978-0-7509-4893-7

Front endpaper: At the start of the century Great Britain was at war in South Africa with the Boers. This group
of volunteers from the Leeds Rifles company (8th battalion West Riding Regiment) parading at Strensall camp,
north of York, in May 1900, was about to embark.
Back endpaper: Map of City Centre attractions.
Half title page: Charter of Queen Victoria, 13 February 1893. The charter conferred the title of a city on
account of 'the antiquity, size and importance of Leeds and other considerations'. It was to have 'all such
rank, liberties, privileges and immunities as are incident to a City'.
Title page: Grant of Arms, 7 November 1921.
The corporation of Leeds had a seal with which to authenticate documents issued in its name since 1626.
Its heraldic device incorporated the fleece and owls which have been recurring elements in the town's coat
of arms ever since. Not until 1921, however, were they formally authorised by the College of Arms. The only
amendments made by the College of Arms were to change the colour of the owls from argent (silver) to proper
(brown) and to add a helmet to the crest.

West Yorkshire
Archive Service

Typeset in Photina.
Typesetting and origination by
Sutton Publishing.
Printed and bound in England.

The West Yorkshire Archive Service is part of
West Yorkshire Joint Services, provided by a
Joint Committee of the Metropolitan Districts
of Bradford, Calderdale, Kirklees, Leeds and
Wakefield.

Contents

The Lord Mayor of the City of Leeds, Councillor Keith Parker, 1999–2000.

LEEDS

Foreword

When I was elected as Lord Mayor of Leeds for the year 1999–2000, I quickly realised what an enormous privilege I had been given. The last time we turned a millennium, Leeds barely existed. If it did, it was a tiny rural community locked in the depths of the Dark-Age forests. Hermits were just beginning to colonise a site that would become the mighty Kirkstall Abbey. Most of Northumbria, of which this area was a part, was at war. But now, as we enter the new millennium, I have the honour of representing one of the UK's fastest-growing economies, a city that can pull its weight on the national and international scene. We are a city of prosperity, opportunity, style and potential. We owe our early growth to coal, textiles and manufacturing. Today our economy is broadly based, diverse and buoyant. We can have confidence in a secure future.

In the pages of this book, we can see Leeds' transformation into a great metropolitan city over the last century. It is a fascinating and informative study. As Leeds' first citizen, I am proud of our long heritage and the cultural and economic richness it brings to our future.

Lord Mayor of the City of Leeds
Councillor Keith Parker

Sixteen-seater Milnes tramcar no. 1 at York Road terminus. *c.* 1900.

Britain: A Century of Change

Children gathered around an early wireless set in the 1920s. The speed and forms of communication were to change dramatically as the century advanced. (*Barnaby's Picture Library*)

T he delirious rejoicing at the news of the Relief of Mafeking, during the Boer War in May 1900, is a colourful historical moment. But, in retrospect, the introduction that year of the first motor bus was rather more important, signalling another major adjustment to town life. In the previous 60 years railway stations, post-and-telegraph offices, police and fire stations, gas works and gasometers, new livestock markets and covered markets, schools, churches, football grounds, hospitals and asylums, water pumping stations and sewerage plants had totally altered the urban scene, as the country's population tripled and over 70 per cent were born in or moved to the towns.

When Queen Victoria died in 1901, she was measured for her coffin by her grandson Kaiser Wilhelm, the London prostitutes put on black mourning and the blinds came down in the villas and terraces spreading out from the old town centres. These centres were reachable by train and tram, by the new bicycles and still newer motor cars, con-nected by the new telephone, and lit by gas or even electricity. The shops may have been full of British-made cotton and woollen clothing but the grocers and butchers were selling cheap Danish bacon, Argentinian beef, Australasian mutton, tinned or dried fish and fruit from Canada, California and South Africa. Most of these goods were carried in British-built-and-crewed ships, burning Welsh steam coal.

As the first decade moved on, the Open Spaces Act meant more parks, bowling greens and cricket pitches. The first state pensions came in, together with higher taxation and death duties. These were raised mostly to pay for the new Dreadnought battleships needed to maintain naval superiority over Germany, and deter them from war. But the deterrent did not work. The First World War transformed the place of women, as they took over many men's jobs. Its other legacies were the war memorials which joined the statues of Victorian worthies in main squares round the land. After 1918 death duties bit even harder and a quarter of England changed hands in a few years.

Women working as porters on the Great Western Railway, Paddington, *c.* 1917. (*W.L. Kenning/ Adrian Vaughan Collection*)

The multiple shop – the chain store – appeared in the high street: Sainsburys, Maypole, Lipton's, Home & Colonial, the Fifty Shilling Tailor, Burton, Boots, W.H. Smith. The shopper was spoilt for choice, attracted by the brash fascias and advertising hoardings for national brands like Bovril, Pears Soap, and Ovaltine. Many new buildings began to be seen, such as garages, motor showrooms, picture palaces (cinemas), 'palais de dance', and the bow-windowed, pebble-dashed, tile-hung, half-timbered houses that were built as ribbon-development along the roads and new bypasses or on the new estates nudging the green belts.

During the 1920s cars became more reliable and sophisticated as well as commonplace, with developments like the electric self-starter making them easier for women to drive. Who wanted to turn a crank handle in the new short skirt? This was, indeed, the electric age as much as the motor era. Trolley buses, electric trams and trains extended mass transport and electric light replaced gas in the street and the home, which itself was groomed by the vacuum cleaner.

A major jolt to the march onward and upward was administered by the Great Depression of the early 1930s. The older British industries – textiles, shipbuilding, iron, steel, coal – were already under pressure from foreign competition when this worldwide slump arrived, cutting exports by half in two years and producing 3 million unemployed (and still rising) by 1932. Luckily there were new diversions to alleviate the misery. The 'talkies' arrived in the cinemas; more and more radios and gramophones were to be found in people's homes; there were new women's magazines, with fashion, cookery tips and problem pages; football pools; the flying feats of women pilots like Amy Johnson; the Loch Ness Monster; cheap chocolate and the drama of Edward VIII's abdication.

Father and child cycling past Buckingham Palace on VE Day, 8 May 1945. (*Hulton Getty Picture Collection*)

Things were looking up again by 1936 and unemployment was down to 2 million. New light industry was booming in the Home Counties as factories struggled to keep up with the demand for radios, radiograms, cars and electronic goods including the first television sets. The threat from Hitler's Germany meant rearmament, particularly of the airforce, which stimulated aircraft and aero engine firms. If you were lucky and lived in the south, there was good money to be earned. A semi-detached house cost £450, a Morris Cowley £150. People may have smoked like chimneys but life expectancy, since 1918, was up by 15 years while the birth rate had almost halved. The fifty-four hour week was down to forty-eight hours and there were 9 million radio licences by 1939.

In some ways it is the little memories that seem to linger longest from the Second World War: the kerbs painted white to show up in the blackout, the rattle of ack-ack shrapnel on roof tiles, sparrows killed by bomb blast, painting your legs brown and then adding a black seam

A family gathered
around their
television set in
the 1950s. (*Hulton
Getty Picture
Collection*)

down the back to simulate stockings. The biggest damage, apart from
London, was in the south-west (Plymouth, Bristol) and the Midlands
(Coventry, Birmingham). Postwar reconstruction was rooted in the
Beveridge Report which set out the expectations for the Welfare State.
This, together with the nationalisation of the Bank of England, coal,
gas, electricity and the railways, formed the programme of the Labour
government in 1945. At this time the USA was calling in its debts and
Britain was beggared by the war, yet still administering its Empire.

Times were hard in the late 1940s, with rationing even more stringent
than during the war. Yet this was, as has been said, 'an innocent and
well-behaved era'. The first let-up came in 1951 with the Festival of
Britain and then there was another fillip in 1953 from the Coronation,
which incidentally gave a huge boost to the spread of TV. By 1954 leisure
motoring had been resumed but the Comet – Britain's best hope for

taking on the American aviation industry – suffered a series of mysterious crashes. The Suez debacle of 1956 was followed by an acceleration in the withdrawal from Empire, which had begun in 1947 with the Independence of India. Consumerism was truly born with the advent of commercial TV and most homes soon boasted washing machines, fridges, electric irons and fires.

The *Lady Chatterley* obscenity trial in 1960 was something of a straw in the wind for what was to follow in that decade. A collective loss of inhibition seemed to sweep the land, as stately home owners opened up, the Beatles and the Rolling Stones transformed popular music, and retailing, cinema and the theatre were revolutionised. Designers, hairdressers, photographers and models moved into places vacated by an Establishment put to flight by the new breed of satirists spawned by *Beyond the Fringe* and *Private Eye*.

In the 1970s Britain seems to have suffered a prolonged hangover after the excesses of the previous decade. Ulster, inflation and union troubles were not made up for by entry into the EEC, North Sea Oil, Women's Lib or, indeed, Punk Rock. Mrs Thatcher applied the corrective in the 1980s, as the country moved more and more from its old manufacturing base over to providing services, consulting, advertising, and expertise in the 'invisible' market of high finance or in IT. Britain entertained the world with *Cats*, *Phantom of the Opera*, *Four Weddings and a Funeral*, *The Full Monty*, *Mr Bean* and the *Teletubbies*.

The post-1945 townscape has seen changes to match those in the worlds of work, entertainment and politics. In 1956 the Clean Air Act served notice on smogs and pea-souper fogs, smuts and blackened buildings, forcing people to stop burning coal and go over to smokeless sources of heat and energy. In the same decade some of the best urban building took place in the 'new towns' like Basildon, Crawley, Stevenage and Harlow. Elsewhere open warfare was declared on slums and what was labelled inadequate, cramped, back-to-back, two-up, two-down, housing. The new 'machine for living in' was a flat in a high-rise block. The architects and planners who promoted these were in league with the traffic engineers, determined to keep the motor car moving whatever the price in multi-storey car parks, meters, traffic wardens and ring roads.

Carnaby Street in the 1960s. (*Barnaby's Picture Library*)

13

The Millennium Dome at Greenwich, 1999. (*Michael Durnan/Barnaby's Picture Library*)

The old pollutant, coal smoke, was replaced by petrol and diesel exhaust, and traffic noise. Even in the back garden it was hard to find peace as motor mowers, then leaf blowers and strimmers made themselves heard, and the neighbours let you share their choice of music from their powerful new amplifiers, whether you wanted to or not. Fast food was no longer only a pork pie in a pub or fish-and-chips. There were Indian curry houses, Chinese take-aways and American-style hamburgers, while the drinker could get away from beer in a wine bar. Under the impact of television the big Gaumonts and Odeons closed or were rebuilt as multi-screen cinemas, while the palais de dance gave way to discos and clubs.

From the late 1960s the introduction of listed buildings and conservation areas, together with the growth of preservation societies, put a brake on 'comprehensive redevelopment'. Now the new risk at the end of the 1990s is that town centres may die, as shoppers are attracted to the edge-of-town supermarkets surrounded by parking space, where much more than food and groceries can be bought. The ease of the one-stop shop represents the latest challenge to the good health of our towns. But with care, ingenuity and a determination to keep control of our environment, this challenge can be met.

Leeds: An Introduction

This century the city of Leeds has grown from a population of 428,968 in 1901 to 706,000 in 1991. It has continued to be a dominant influence on the Yorkshire and Humberside region. The city has benefited from its location at a point where the valleys of the eastern flowing rivers of the Wharfe and Aire emerge from the Pennine uplands and flow out on to the Vale of York. The city has also spread geographically, absorbing neighbouring communities. In 1974 it took control of all the adjoining district councils. But it has lost population from the central core to outlying areas, although this process has begun to reverse recently. Over the last ten years the city has experienced a regeneration. Today it is the fastest growing city in Britain. One hundred thousand people work in the city centre. There is a potential workforce of 1.9 million people within a 30-mile radius of the city. This has attracted, and continues to attract, new businesses. During the academic year the population of students alone reaches over 90,000. This in turn has stimulated the growth of bars and night clubs.

A resident who left the city in 1900 and returned in 1999 would recognise little of the place he once knew. Great public buildings like the Town Hall, the Corn Exchange, the Parish Church, St John's, Briggate, and the Grand Theatre would stand out in streets that had changed almost beyond recognition. The completion of City Square in 1903, the rebuilding of Kirkgate Market in 1904, would have taken place later. While to a large extent the pattern of streets at the core remains almost unaltered, their surroundings have been transformed. The pace of remodelling has been steady as the century has progressed. City centre streets, like Guildford Street (the Headrow) and Cookridge Street, have been widened to improve traffic flow. The area around the newly built Civic Hall has been transformed. Swathes of the city have been demolished for the inner ring road, and new housing developments have appeared. Magnificent eighteenth-century buildings like Brooke House, in Hunslet, and Bischoff House, in North Street have been lost. Impressive office blocks like the Royal Exchange and Standard House in City Square have been demolished along with Beckett's Bank. This

1912 Meanwood valley in the snow. A pastoral scene, the site famous for a civil war skirmish in Batty's wood, only a mile and a half from the city centre. After the First World War the farmland around the model farm on the left of the picture was to be developed into the Sugarwell housing estate. On the right-hand side the Woodlands Dye Works was to be demolished in the 1970s. Groves mill became a factory and the site is now a growing housing development along Meanwood Road.

very ancient resident would be amazed, of course, to see the revolution in the health, education and general prosperity of the population. And be transported by the noise and activity of the shopping crowds. They would be bewildered by the way in which electricity and the telephone have infiltrated every aspect of life. They would be terrified by the speed and appearance of the traffic on the roads and astounded by the noise of the jet planes landing at Leeds and Bradford Airport.

At the end of the twentieth century, it would be all too easy for this resident to look back over 100 years of the history of Leeds and imagine that it was one of seamless progress. Yet some 40 years elapsed before the good intentions of the city council, in establishing the Quarry Hill Unhealthy Area, were translated into positive action. Only then did they create the impressive housing experiment that was Quarry Hill flats. But within ten years this achievement was undermined by structural problems, which ultimately resulted in total demolition. Public housing has since gone round in circles. The much vilified back-to-back housing that has typified Leeds has not been entirely eradicated, but where it survives, has been brought up to an acceptable modern standard. Two world wars have disrupted all attempts at long-term planning. The public transport system dependent on the noisy and dirty tram, was finally abandoned in 1959. Yet plans for the next century include the Supertram (the rapid transit system for the city).

Those whose experience of the city is more recent, perhaps of only the last 20 years, might have difficulty imagining the grime-covered

1910 Moortown, in Moor Allerton parish, was another satellite village in the city that retained its rustic charm and rural isolation. The church in the distance is St John's, built in 1852. The village burgeoned into a residential suburb after the Second World War.

buildings that were until recently the most obvious reminders of its industrial past. The long and difficult battle to cleanse the city has been as much about economic change as about public health. While the prosperity of the city depended on coal-fired factories and the only means of heating your home was a coal fire, the atmosphere of Leeds would continue to be blighted. The postwar decline in the diverse manufacturing base has meant a gradual reduction in demand for coal. Homes have been increasingly heated by non-coal-based sources. Legislation to control smoke emissions accompanied this process. By the 1970s the last of the big engineering firms like Greenwood & Batley and Fairbairn Lawson fell victim to the current fashion for asset stripping. For almost 20 years many factory sites remained in expectation of development. The recession of the 1980s took time to abate. Yet in recent years the new financial and legal services and new technology like the Internet, and such developments as call centres, have begun to provide new employment opportunities. At the same time the city has begun to address its potential as a tourist resort, and cater for visitors in a way it has never done before.

1910 Crossgates station, the Leeds platform. Crossgates was a desirable country location with ready access to the city but did not begin to become part of the city until 1912. The photograph is by J.W. Hague, a newsagent in Crossgates.

At the end of the century it is instructive to look back at some of these changes through the eyes of those who were there at the time. Photographs of events in the past century reveal much about the way the city appeared to contemporaries. A photograph is a record of a fleeting moment and yet, at its best, it is also a record of so much more; of buildings long since demolished, fashion long forgotten, people frozen in time, and a way of life. The photographs here range from the work of some of the best professional photographers to a variety of keen amateurs. Most were taken as a deliberate record of an event for a customer, for sale or for future reference. All contribute to an insight into a century of Leeds.

The Start of the Century

1903   Buffalo Bill, W.F. Cody, brought his *Wild West Show and Congress of Rough Riders* with 800 men and 500 horses to Cardigan Fields, Leeds, from 28 September to 3 October as part of a major tour of the country. This was his second and last visit to the city but the remarkable spectacle was to be remembered by those that saw it as children into their old age. His show defined an era of American history for the world. When he died, on 10 January 1917, the news eclipsed that of events during the First World War.

1900 An unusual view of the audience at a performance in the City Varieties Music Hall, Swan Street, now Leeds City Varieties, famous for presenting the BBC TV show *The Good Old Days*. It ran from 1953 to 1983 and is the longest-running TV music show. The theatre was one of seven in the city at this time providing a range of live entertainment. One, the Coliseum, did not long survive the attractions of animated pictures which it began showing in 1905.

21

1900 The entrance to the Midland Railway, Wellington Street station, one of three stations in Leeds at this time. The others were 'Central', the Great Northern Railway station, and 'New', the North Eastern Railway station. Most long-distance travel was undertaken by rail. A bus service to London was just beginning its commercial operation. Horses were being superseded and motor cars were not yet efficient or cheap enough. Trams provided for most transport needs around the city; some were still horse drawn, and there were also horse-drawn hackney cabs.

1902 At the top of Briggate, 56 Grand Arcade, Jones Sewing Machine Shop, now a nightclub, the city crowd celebrated victory in the Boer War. Peace Day was 1 June. A portrait of Lord Roberts, the commander-in-chief, has a prominent place. (*McKenna collection in Leeds Central Library*)

1908 His Majesty King Edward VII, accompanied by Queen Alexandra and the Princess Victoria, visited the city to open new university buildings, 7 July. Four years earlier he had incorporated the Yorkshire College by Royal Charter as the University of Leeds. During the academic year 1907–8 there was a total of 800 day students.

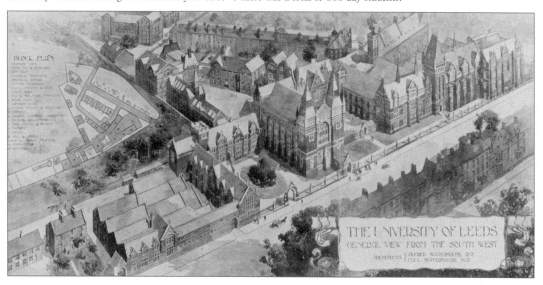

1908 The architect's impression of the layout of the University of Leeds after the construction of the new accommodation. The main new buildings were to house the Electrical Engineering and the Mining, Metallurgical, Gas and Fuel departments. The university has steadily enlarged in the area of Little Woodhouse over the century with new buildings and by adapting the existing domestic housing stock. At 5 De Grey Road, in this complex, the famous chidren's writer Arthur Ransome was born.

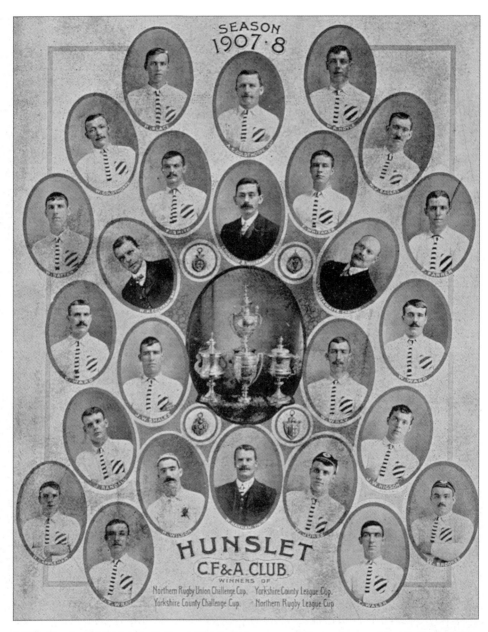

1908 The Hunslet Cricket, Football and Athletic Club was one of the most successful rugby football clubs in the new Northern Union after the rift which had taken place within the English Rugby Union in 1898. Players in Lancashire and Yorkshire worked on Saturdays and clubs paid compensation to them which offended against the amateur status of other players. The division between Union and League was born and has continued almost to the end of the century. Since 1995 the Union game has been 'open'.

1906 Schofield's store at no. 1 Victoria Arcade. Snowden Schofield opened his first shop in 1901 and by 1906 had purchased the whole of one side of the arcade. By 1947 he controlled the whole arcade. This process of expansion created a major department store in a prime location, and added to the attractions of Leeds as a shopping destination.

1911 The Red Hall, the most prominent seventeenth-century building in the city centre, purchased by Snowden Schofield in 1912. Built in 1628, it was famous as the place of captivity of King Charles I in 1647, before his transfer to London and execution. Mr Schofield lovingly restored the building and turned it into a café for the store. However after his death in 1949, the whole site was redeveloped between 1957 and 1962. The Red Hall was demolished in 1961.

1904 A practical cookery class in the Leeds School of Cookery and Domestic Economy in Albion Street. Popularly known as the 'Pud School' it was founded by the Yorkshire Ladies Council of Education in 1874. In 1907 it became the responsibility of the Leeds Education Committee. As the Yorkshire Training College of Housecraft it moved to premises in Vernon Road in 1933. It is now part of Leeds Metropolitan University.

1907 West Leeds Boys' High School, Whingate Road, was one of the first secondary schools to be built by the Leeds Education Committee under the 1902 Education Act. This is one of a series of excellent photographs taken to record the range of classes taught. A woodworking class learned about the character of different woods. The school was built to cater for a total of some 600 pupils. This building was closed in 1992.

1905 Sir James Kitson, outside his house Gledhow Hall, about to be taken for a spin in his grandson Roland's new motor. Sir James was one of the leading industrialists of his age. He was chairman of the family firm, Kitson & Company Limited, Airedale Foundry and the Monkbridge Iron and Steel Works. These were typical of the companies that provided the basis of the wealth of the city. He had sat as a Liberal MP for the Colne Valley from 1892 to 1907 when he was raised to the peerage as Lord Airedale.

1907 Lord Airedale in his study at Gledhow Hall. He was to die unexpectedly in Paris, on 16 March 1911, while on holiday. His estate was provisionally valued at £1 million. It was believed to be the fourteenth estate of such size in the country to provide a windfall for the Treasury in that year. Death duties had been introduced in 1896, and £150,000 had to be paid out of the estate to the Inland Revenue authorities.

27

1903 Victor H. Watson (1878–1943), printer and entrepreneur. At this time he was working for the printers, Goodall & Suddick. The portrait was taken four years before he joined John Waddington Ltd as lithographic foreman. He subsequently took over the management of the ailing firm. In the process he turned it from a little-known printer of theatre posters into the leading games publisher in the country. He made 'Monopoly' a household name.

1905 Hunslet Lake. This feature was filled in in 1908 when the Hunslet Lake Amateur Bowling Club applied to the city council for a further green.

1905 Quarry Mount Boys' School football team. This year they won the School Football Association's Challenge Cup, beating Kirkstall St Stephens in the final. The photograph was taken by the headmaster, Samuel Crowther, a keen amateur photographer.

1905 Hunslet Feast with a popular feature, the 'Ride of the Present Day'. This event was one of the many feasts around the city that enabled local people to enjoy a break from the daily round of work.

1911 Roundhay Park and a band performance; in the background stands Roundhay Mansion. The bandstand almost seems to symbolise the Edwardian era as a golden age of leisure. Such bandstands flourished throughout the parks of Leeds during the period 1906–14.

1911 Trainee teachers receiving practical experience at Quarry Mount Boys School. Back row, left to right: Messrs Scarborough, Wolton, Boyes, Gilbert, Waller; front row: Messrs Appleby, Kerr (tutor) and Southworth. The City of Leeds Training College was opened in 1907 in the former home of the Leeds Girls' High School in Woodhouse Lane. New purpose-built premises at Beckett's Park were opened in 1913 and now form part of Leeds Metropolitan University.

1911 Children dressed for camp in the playground of Czar Street Industrial School. The central figure is that of Mrs H. Currer Briggs, widow of another leading industrialist and coal owner, Arthur Currer Briggs of Gledhow Grange. Active in many areas of good works she was a prime mover in enabling poor children to experience the health and freedom of a holiday by the sea. The Leeds Poor Children's Holiday Camp Association had a holiday home at Silverdale on Morecambe Bay.

1906 One of the first tramcars from Leeds to Rodley at 5.30 a.m. on 9 July, no. 155. The veracity of the information on this photograph has been questioned by Jim Soper in his monumental history of Leeds transport. The manuscript daily report for 9 July shows that the first car which left the depot for Rodley at 4.48 a.m. was no. 156. The track was laid by unemployed labour. There was a severe gradient on Whitecote Hill and trams had to observe a speed limit of 4 mph on this stretch. Gradually Leeds City Tramways began providing more and more services beyond the city boundary.

1911 An illuminated tramcar celebrating the coronation of George V. It had its own special timetable for touring the city. This enterprising development by Leeds City Tramways Department, of illuminating tramcars, was an inspiration for other municipal departments throughout the country.

The First World War

1914 The outbreak of the war was accompanied by the belief that it would be short. Life went on much as normal, but unemployment rose as firms reduced their hours in response to the drop in consumer activity. More military men were seen in the streets, however. This shot of Bond Street shows sailors spilling out on to Albion Street between the music shop of J.W. Sykes and the jewellers, Pearce & Son. The latter shop was to become the main office of the *Yorkshire Post*, although the new headquarters had been established in 8 Change Court since 1866, at the rear of Bond Street.

1914 At Leeds University the members of the Officer Training Corps lined up to attest their loyalty to the crown and volunteer for action. A total of 1,204 cadets passed through the university contingent during the course of the war.

1914 Victoria Hall, Leeds Town Hall, where Leeds University students were drafted in to assist the city council administration. They were compiling the city section of the National Register of men and women available for war work.

Lieut. J. B. Gawthorpe.   Lieut. L. C. Hossell.   Lieut. The Hon. R. D. Kitson.   Capt. R. Salter.   Quarter-Master and Hon. Lieut. Boult.   Lieut. R. M. Waddington.

Lieut. H. A. Adams.   Lieut. A. ap Ellis.   Capt. Arnold Wilson.   Capt. S. S. Sykes.   Capt. T. Longbottom.

Capt. E. W. Braithwaite.   Lieut. W. H. Greenwood.   Capt. F. A. Lupton.   Capt. W. Derry.   Capt. Andrew Wilson.   2nd Lieut. S. H. Elkington.   2nd Lieut. D. A. Powys.

Capt. W. H. Brooke.   Lieut. C. Hartnell.   Major J. W. Alexander, T.D.   Lt.-Colonel E. Kitson Clark, T.D.   Capt. and Adjutant A. C. Dundas.   Major R. A. Hudson.

1914 Officers of the 8th Battalion (Leeds Rifles), The Prince of Wales's Own (West Yorkshire Regiment). This group of territorial officers were at their usual summer camp at Strensall awaiting orders.

1914 Harry Exley, a teacher, with three scholarship winners at Quarry Mount Boys' School. From left to right they were Alf Davies, Victor Hodgson and Cyril Ramsden. Gaining a Junior City Scholarship ensured that pupils could continue their education, after twelve years of age, at a council secondary school, without having to pay the fees.

1915 A view of 88 Pontefract Lane, the home and office of James Thomas Thackray, chimney sweep. Whether at war or peace the homes of Leeds were almost entirely heated by coal fires and gave employment to a large number of sweeps. The consequent pollution was an endemic public health problem. Outside the house stand the chimney brush and the bag of soot.

1915 120 Marsh Lane, Mathers, outfitters. This picture was taken on 25 February along the route of the proposed Thorpe Stapleton sewage disposal scheme. Above the shop windows are signs that a major world war was under way, with recruitment posters encouraging men to enrol.

1915   A corner shop in Green Street, Burmantofts, with everything the housewife of the age could desire. A dolly hangs from the doorframe, along with frying pans, and a washboard stands on the pavement.

1915   Another local shop in Burmantofts, I. Mollett, greengrocer, 35 Green Road. There is a wide range of produce on display, including skinned rabbits, hanging from a board outside.

1915 Charles Lupton, Lord Mayor of Leeds 1915–16. A leading lawyer in the city, he was also prominent in efforts to improve the hospital provision and the road system. During his mayoralty he actively raised £150,000 to complete the extension of Leeds General Infirmary, begun before the war. He also raised £25,000 for additional temporary accommodation at Beckett's Park Military Hospital. After the war he was the driving force behind the schemes to widen the Headrow, create the outer ring road and the arterial road system.

1915 Charles Richard Hattersley Pickard, of 2nd Battalion Leeds Volunteer Training Corps at Monk Fryston Camp at Whitsuntide. He was a commercial photographer, living at Crossgates. He volunteered to serve even though in his mid-forties. His business in Kirkgate was to dominate commercial photography in the city for most of the century. He died in 1972, in his 100th year.

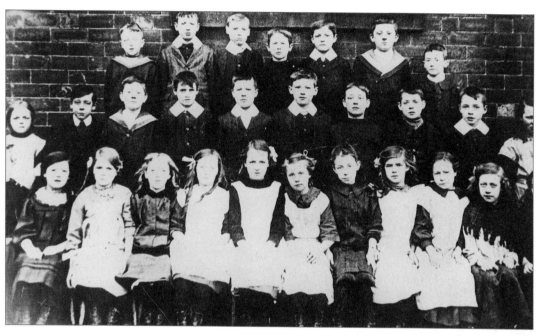

1916 Middleton Village School catering for a small mining community on the southern outskirts of the city, which was not part of the city until 1919. It was not until after the Second World War that Leeds City Council established the Middleton estate. There they rehoused many families from some of the thousands of demolished back-to-back houses, for which Leeds was notorious.

1916 Broom Pit, Middleton Colliery Fireclay works. The staff were assembled for a commemorative photograph. In the foreground stands a model of the Matthew Murray locomotive that was run on the Middleton railway from the colliery to the coal staithe on the River Aire in 1812.

1915 King George V visited East Leeds War Hospital (Leeds Workhouse Infirmary, later St James's Hospital), part of the 2nd Northern General Hospital, on 28 September. More and more civilian buildings were appropriated to war use as trench warfare brought increasing casualties. He talked with the wounded and decorated Private Preston of 6th Battalion West Yorkshire Regiment with the DCM.

1915 Staff of the Great Northern Railway station on the eve of the sinking of the great Cunard liner the *Lusitania*. One thousand four hundred men, women and children died after the ship was torpedoed without warning by a German submarine on 7 May. Americans had been warned not to sail. This event contributed to bringing the United States into the war against Germany. The newspaper stand poster reads 'Lusitania bookable'.

1918 Lotherton Hall, the home of the Gascoigne family, in use as a Voluntary Aid Detachment convalescent hospital. Now the hall is a popular country house museum with a costume gallery and bird garden run by Leeds City Museum and Art Galleries Service.

1918 Killingbeck Municipal Sanatorium with the isolation wards in use for soldiers. The hospital was built in 1913 on the Killingbeck Hall estate. This had been purchased by the city council in 1898 from the Hon. Mrs Meynell Ingram of Temple Newsam. The hall was demolished in 1978.

1917 Lance-Corporal Walker who was awarded the Military Medal for gallantry, when serving with the Middlesex Yeomanry in the Salonika forces. He was a former pupil of West Leeds High School.

Between the Wars

1919 Sir John McLaren, President of Leeds Chamber of Commerce. He
was awarded the KBE for his services to the improvement of provision of
munitions during the war. As chairman of the Board of Control set up by
the Ministry of Munitions he pioneered the establishment in Armley of
the first National Ordnance shell factory in England. He followed it with
a larger one at Barnbow. His experience as a successful engineer and co-
founder, with his brother Henry, of the agricultural machinery and steam
plough manufacturers at Midland Engine Works, Jack Lane, Hunslet, was
the essential foundation of his influence.

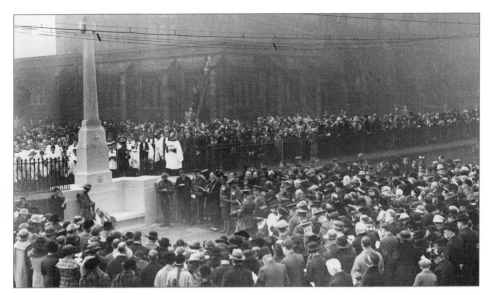

1921 The unveiling of the war memorial to the men of the 7th and 8th Battalions West Yorkshire Regiment (Leeds Rifles), on 13 November, at Leeds Parish Church in Kirkgate. An estimated crowd of some 20,000, including troops, relatives of the fallen and members of the general public were present. The Portland stone memorial was designed by Sir Edwin Lutyens. The memorial was unveiled by Captain G. Sanders VC, MC (who enlisted in the Rifles as a private in 1914 and was one of nine VCs from the city during the war).

1922 The Earl of Harewood unveiled the city war memorial in City Square on 10 October. He was dressed in the uniform of a major. There was no guard of honour, no military pomp or display. Twenty to thirty thousand people were present to hear his lordship say that 'the individual part in the war was a very minute one but the collective part was vital and of the greatest'. Out of a population of 450,000 some 90,000 men had joined the forces and more than 10,000 made the supreme sacrifice. The memorial, by Henry Charles Fehr, was repositioned in the newly created Garden of Rest on the Headrow in the 1930s.

1922 The 10,000th child to be sent for a holiday at Silverdale by the Leeds Poor Children's Holiday Camp Association, since the camp opened in 1904. She was presented with a bouquet of flowers at Central station. Mrs Helen Currer Briggs stands in the midst of the children with the Lady Mayoress, Mrs Fountain. An interesting statistic was reported: this was that as the average increase of weight for each child over the holiday was roughly 3lb, then since 1904 the association had contributed some 15 tons to the weight of the population of Leeds!

1923 Holbeck Amateur Swimming Club water polo team, the champions for that year in Leeds District. The success of the men and the popularity of swimming led to demands for the formation of a Ladies Swimming Club in 1926. Fifty ladies turned up to the meeting at Holbeck Public Laundry on 11 October and formed a club the same night. Councillor H. Morris commented that 'although the meeting was held in a wash house he was glad to see that it was not a wash out'.

1923 Temple Newsam House was opened to the public on 19 October by the Minister of Labour, Sir Montague Barlow. The house and 913 acres of land had been purchased by Leeds City Council from the Hon. Edward Wood, so that it might be preserved in perpetuity as a national monument. The grounds had already been partially developed for public recreation. Among those present, second to the right of the Lord Mayor, Alderman Frank Fountain, was the chairman of the Temple Newsam Estate Committee, Alderman Sir Charles Wilson MP, who has gone down in local history as the 'man who was Leeds', as he claimed during a public enquiry. He served as Conservative council leader, and was the leading force in local government from 1908 to 1926.

1926 Leeds Tercentenary Celebrations 8–17 July. A series of events marked the city's progress from receiving its first charter of incorporation as a municipal borough on 13 July 1626. In the background of this view of City Square is a replica of the old Moot Hall, built over the entrance of Wellington station by the London Midland & Scottish Railway Company. The Moot Hall stood in the middle of Briggate and was demolished in 1825. This photograph is by Harold G. Grainger FRPS, who specialised in rather soft focus pictures.

1926 Leeds Tercentenary Celebrations. On 11 July the Lord Mayor, Councillor J. Arnott, JP processed with the civic party through the specially erected Kirkgate Bar, to a Service of Thanksgiving at Leeds Parish Church. The battlemented arch at the junction with Vicar Lane was provided by the tradesmen of Kirkgate.

1926 Lt-Colonel Edwin Kitson Clark, chairman of Kitsons, the engineering firm, held a garden party for members of Leeds Parish Church at his home, Meanwoodside. He is on the left of the picture with his wife. His wide interests included serving in the Leeds Rifles and acting as Vicar's warden at the Parish Church. He was behind the establishment of the Leeds Civic Society in 1918 'to promote good taste, encourage cultivated recreation and assist the cause of health'.

1926 A view across the rooftops of Leeds during the General Strike. The Corn Exchange, built in 1855, is in the foreground and St Mary's, Richmond Hill, on the horizon. Between them stands the tower of Leeds Parish Church. One factory chimney belches smoke but the lack of activity from the many others was, apparently, the prime reason for the existence of this scene. The unusual clarity of the air made a photograph worth taking.

1926 View of Kirkgate Market. The impressive building, designed by Leeming & Leeming, was opened in 1904. It has been sympathetically restored in recent years. In the centre of the background rises St Mary's Quarry Hill, demolished in 1977.

1927 The new millinery department in Leeds Industrial Cooperative Society's flagship store in Albion Street. The Society was celebrating its 80th anniversary and branching out into competition with other major retailers like Schofields. The store was rebuilt in the 1960s but was recently sold for development.

1927 The 100th Cooperative Society branch store opened in Chapeltown Road. The quality building survives and now houses the offices of the Chapeltown Enterprise Centre.

1927 Kirkstall Abbey Museum was opened on 11 July by the Lord Mayor, Hugh Lupton, accompanied by the Lady Mayoress, Mrs E. Lupton. The building had been left to Leeds Corporation by Col. J.T. Harding. Concentrating on exhibits relating to everyday life in the past, it has long required improvements. These are now being provided by a major redevelopment project funded by the Heritage Lottery Fund.

1928 Armley Babies' Welcome was opened by the Princess Royal on 9 August. The old Town Street School had been made available by Armley Common Rights Trust for the purpose. The Princess was accompanied by Mrs Kitson Clark, on the left, retiring President, and Mrs Blackburn, President 1926–56. There was a guard of honour of mothers with babies in prams. The first Babies' Welcome was opened in Ellerby Road in 1909 to offer training for mothers in the rearing and management of their babies, and to combat the high infant mortality of the age.

1929 J. Ramsay Macdonald MP addressing an audience of over 15,000 people in North Street Recreation Ground, Leeds, on Saturday 25 May. He claimed to have the other two parties, the Liberals and Conservatives on the run. A few days later he formed the second minority Labour government. In the Leeds Central constituency the sitting Conservative MP, Sir Charles Wilson, was defeated by the Hon. R.D. Denman for Labour. The photograph is by Alf Mattison.

1929   Hunslet Carr with the recreation ground and bowling green in the centre, Claytons, engineers and manufacturers of gasholders in the north-east, the rows of the 'gasholders' and then the 'Arthingtons', streets of back-to-back houses. On the southern edge of the recreation ground can be seen the Hunslet Carr Glassworks. The whole area has been transformed by the construction of the M1 into the city centre.

1933   Leeds Civic Hall. Along with Quarry Hill flats and the Queens Hotel, built some years later, this was the most significant building in the city centre between the wars. Designed by E. Vincent Harris, with twin towers 170 ft high each surmounted by a large gilt owl, the impressive interior provides for three separate functions. There is a ceremonial block with reception and banqueting halls and Lord Mayor's room, a Council Chamber with ante-room and members' rooms, and two ranges of administrative offices.

1933 Opening of Leeds Civic Hall, August. King George V inspects the guard of honour with Brigadier Kenneth Hargreaves outside the Town Hall, before proceeding to the new building. The Town Hall, designed by Cuthbert Brodrick and opened by Queen Victoria on 7 September 1858, had long since ceased to provide adequate accommodation for local government. Ironically, however, the building has come to symbolise municipal government for the media.

1933 The monument to Brooke Hall, which was built in about 1670 by Alderman Thomas Kitchingman, Mayor of Leeds in 1688 and 1705 and occupied by another alderman and mayor, John Brooke, in the eighteenth century. It was unveiled by the Lord Mayor, Alderman R.H. Blackburn, who described the site as the birthplace of many Leeds industries. Built with bricks from the recently demolished building the monument reflected the desire of many Leeds folk to preserve something of their historic past under pressure from commercial development. The efforts of the antiquarian E. Kilburn Scott encouraged the Anglo-American Oil Company to provide the monument near to the site of the building at the junction of Hunslet Lane and South Brooke Street, now an access road to the M1 and M621. The monument partially survives today, adjoining the Esso service station in Meadow Lane. The original bricks disappeared after the site was redeveloped in 1975.

1936 The Duke of Devonshire, Chancellor of the University of Leeds, speaking at the opening of the Brotherton Library on 6 October. The library was declared open by the Archbishop of Canterbury, Dr Lang, who had served at Leeds Parish Church as a curate. He described the library as 'a great reservoir where the great waters of knowledge are stored and from which the stream will flow out to laboratory, lecture room and study'.

1936 Brotherton Library reading room, before being occupied by students. It has 6,000 shelves, enough to hold 200,000 volumes. The huge circular reading room has a diameter of 20 ft, larger than that of the British Museum, and is ringed by twenty pillars of pale green Scandinavian marble. The major part of the cost of this building was contributed by Lord Brotherton.

1934 Workers leaving Burtons Hudson Road factory. The major industrial success in Leeds of the inter-war period and the largest single employer. Burtons employed 8,400 people in the Leeds factory, producing 100,000 complete garments in a week. Employment conditions were the best in the city. There was a large canteen, rest rooms and medical, optical and dental services to enable workers to be as content and, consequently, as productive as possible. Burtons today is part of the Arcadia Group.

1936 Sir Montague Burton with Lady Burton saying goodbye to their granddaughter, Evelyn Beddington Behrens, before they left London for America on 20 August. Montague Burton's rise from poor Jewish refugee to millionaire industrialist was one of the most remarkable achievements of the century.

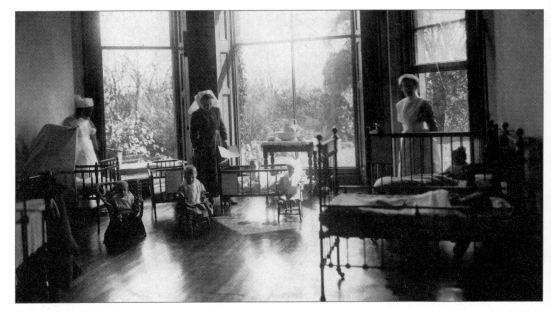

1934 'Eleanor' ward of the Wyther Park Infants Hospital. The hospital was opened as a charitable enterprise by the Lady Mayoress in 1913 but could not be continued on that basis. Leeds Babies' Welcome could not take the hospital on so Leeds City Council Health Committee supported it from 1914 onwards. The hospital concentrated on the needs of children under five years of age. During the war it evacuated to Knaresborough.

1936 Opening of the Killingbeck Sanatorium extension by G. Shakespeare MP, Parliamentary Secretary to the Minister of Health, 9 July. A last-ditch attempt made to list the building on the 89-acre site was not successful. Killingbeck Hospital finally closed in 1997.

1937   The Leeds City Council Housing Committee at Quarry Hill flats on 3 June without their influential Labour chairman, Revd Charles Jenkinson. This massive development of working-class housing, the biggest in Europe, was an innovative scheme, inspired by Vienna's Karl Marx Hof. Built on the site of a Victorian slum area it had taken nearly 40 years to provide new homes. Ultimately over 3,000 people were to be housed in the monumental complex of some 938 flats.

1938   Visitors queued in New York Road to see Quarry Hill flats, 5 April. The first stage in the construction of the flats was completed in March. Potential residents wanted to see the size of the rooms, the electric lighting and gas cooking facilities, and the Garchey automatic waste disposal system. As costly structural problems developed it was decided to demolish the structure in 1973. It took some years to effect. Quarry House, the West Yorkshire Playhouse and the Leeds College of Music occupy the site today.

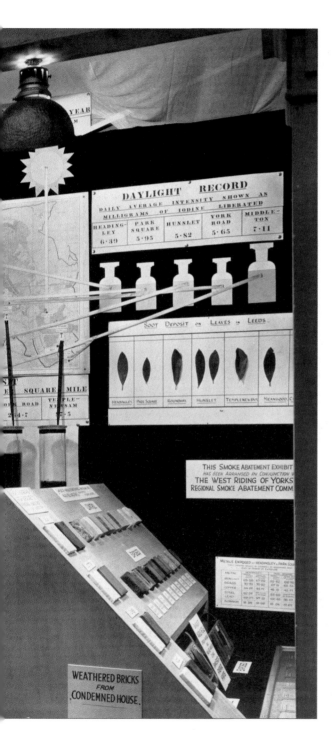

1934 Public Health Exhibition, 17–26 September. This display is perhaps the most revealing photograph of the atmospheric conditions in the city during the inter-war period. Despite the best efforts of the West Riding of Yorkshire Regional Smoke Abatement Committee, the average annual deposit of soot in Park Square was 344.7 tons per square mile, compared with 108.5 tons per square mile in Headingley. It was not until the passage of the Clean Air Act in 1956 that smoke control measures, compelling the use of only smokeless fuel, were to be introduced into the city. Today the air pollution is less visible.

1933 Bishop Cowgill celebrated his jubilee in the priesthood on 20 May. The Roman Catholic Cathedral of St Anne's, designed by John Henry Eastwood, was rebuilt as a result of the widening of Guildford Street and Cookridge Street in 1904. Despite all efforts the cathedral was saddled with debts which were not paid off until 1924 when Bishop Cowgill performed the 4-hour long consecration ceremony.

1937 An Austin 20 hp ambulance was put into commission by the City Council Public Health Department for general cases on 12 October. This purchase marked the unification of the municipal ambulance service under the Health Committee. Previously ambulances had been controlled by three separate committees of the corporation, the Watch (accidents and sudden illness in streets, workshops), Health (maternity, tuberculosis and infectious diseases cases) and Public Assistance (accidents and illness cases removed to municipal general hospitals, lunacy and mental illness).

The Second World War

1939 Jimmy Waite, photographer with Ledbetters, in a gas mask taking a photograph. Gas masks were issued to everyone and were supposed to be carried at all times. Air raid precautions brought home the seriousness of war, but there was always the funny side.

1939 A recruitment hut in City Square with the Queens Hotel, completed only two years before, in the background.

1939 An anti-aircraft gun being moved down Woodhouse Lane. Like the photograph above it is one of Alf Mattison's records of life in the city.

1939 A Mobile First Aid Post in a converted bus at the rear of Leeds General Infirmary. This was one of four such buses operating in the city. It was staffed by eight full-time male and forty-three full-time female staff.

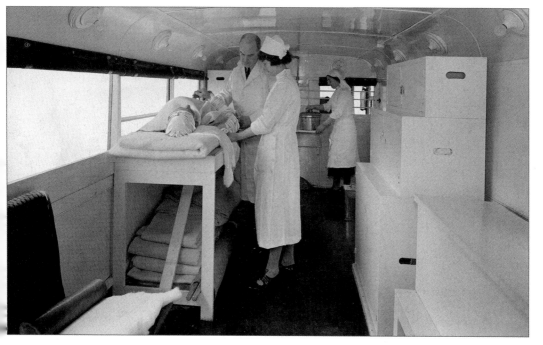

1939 The upper floor of the bus in use.

1940   Bramley Bowling Club. From left to right: Richard Waite, Nathaniel Marshall, John William Dawson and Leonard Pickles. This club was founded in 1907. Despite the war there was still time for relaxation. Mr Dawson even published a short history of the club in 1942, when there was a wartime paper shortage!

1941   Air raid damage in the infants'classroom of Leeds St Peter's School after the raid on the night of 14 March. The Vicar of Leeds, Canon W.M. Askwith inspected the damage with the caretaker. The only casualty was the caretaker's dog. (*Yorkshire Post*)

1941 Air raid damage with an Anderson shelter. The worst raid of the few that were made on Leeds was on the night of 14/15 March. Houses in Gipton, Headingley Woodhouse and Roundhay Road were damaged or destroyed. In all some 7,623 houses were damaged in the raids and only 197 buildings destroyed. But 77 people were killed and 327 injured.

1940 Vesper Gate Drive with a group of people waiting for a tram to take them into the city. Wartime restrictions put a stop to speculative house building but many houses were built between the wars for the salaried middle classes. Low interest rates in the 1930s produced a boom in private house building. Although not enough to satisfy demand they provided new standards of accommodation and comfort.

1941 Staff at the Chapeltown tram depot with women recruits. When the depot was rebuilt in 1908 it was found that the entrance was too narrow for trams to enter. Some rapid demolition was called for.

1942 West Leeds Girls' High School Aid to China sale on 5 December. Japan's entry into the war in December 1941 made nationalist China an ally and voluntary bodies rallied round to help the Aid to China Fund.

1942 West Leeds Girls' High School toy making for air raid victims. They were made by girls of all ages for the Red Cross to distribute to children in bombed areas. This project started off as a hobby and became very popular with the girls. They made 800 toys for charities at a time when toys were very expensive in the shops.

1939 West Leeds High School evacuation picnic at Tadcaster. Mass evacuation took place as soon as war was declared but the lack of air raids during the phoney war encouraged most parents to have their children brought back to the city.

1942 West Leeds High School girls potato picking. Home food production was vital as a result of the blockade of shipping. All hands were needed with the harvest.

1940 A Fairey Swordfish. This multi-role aircraft for the Royal Navy was originally designed in 1934 and was approaching obsolescence in 1939. It nevertheless became one of the most versatile and best-loved aeroplanes of the war. Called the 'stringback' it was used on aircraft carriers. Built under contract by Blackburn Aircraft Ltd, Olympia Works, Roundhay Road, it was subcontracted to adaptable engineering firms in the city including Hudswell Clarke & Co., Thomas Green & Sons Ltd, Appleyards (of Leeds) and Tate of Leeds Ltd.

1942 Fairbairn Lawson's Wellington Street works, where 2-pounder gun barrels were being manufactured by teams of women war workers. There were 600,000 voluntary women workers but they were not enough, so the government made part-time war work compulsory for women. In May 1943 women of eighteen to forty-five had to undertake war work of up to 30 hours a week.

1942 A vehicle manufactured by C.H. Roe Ltd for the services. It had collapsible sides. When opened out it formed a spacious workroom able to contain printing presses and other equipment for producing maps in the field.

1944 J.B. Priestley, the writer and broadcaster, opened the *Yorkshire Evening News* 'Homes of Tomorrow' exhibition in Lewis's department store in the Headrow on 22 June. He said that there were signs that housewives would soon be able to escape from the dilemma of being slaves to the kitchen. Many criticised this sort of exhibition in wartime, but he was in favour.

***c*. 1943** Alf Mattison (1868–1944) was a devoted local historian, and staunch Labour supporter. Much of our knowledge of Leeds during his lifetime is due to his work recording old buildings before demolition, with his camera. He published *The Romance of Old Leeds* as early as 1908. He was known affectionately by his workmates in the City Tramways department as 'Old Leeds'.

71

1939 William Holmes (56), an unemployed miner, at dinner with his family in Quarry Hill flats. He was one of the earliest tenants as the flats were not fully let until the 1940s. A main condition for a tenancy until 1949 was that tenants should be members of the working classes.

1946 Quarry Hill flats looking westwards up the Headrow, an impressive picture of the total development.

1944 Snowden Schofield (1870–1949), when he was President of the Leeds Tradesmen's Benevolent Association. He created a major department store in the Headrow, now the site of the Headrow Shopping Centre. Aged 30 he had left his job as lace buyer for Owen Owen at Liverpool, and started, in his Victoria Arcade shop, by selling lace and fancy drapery.

73

1945 The Prime Minister, Winston Churchill, visited the city, on the election trail, with his wife, Clementine, on 26 June. Twenty-five thousand people turned out to see the great war leader in front of the Civic Hall. In the background the windows of Leeds General Infirmary were lined with nurses and medical students. He spoke for ten minutes urging that this was not the time for a great change. However, the election result gave Labour an overwhelming majority.

1945 VJ celebrations outside Leeds Town Hall on 16 August. Britain learned of the total surrender of Japan at around midnight on 14 August. The government declared a two-day holiday.

Postwar Leeds

1947 A model poses in City Square in an ensemble based on the New Look, created by Christian Dior. It was symbolic of the break with the drab utility clothing of wartime. Square shoulders were out, and a new more feminine shape was in.

***c.* 1949** Low Briggate with trams, cars and a steam engine leaving Leeds City station. In the background is the steeple of Holy Trinity Church. The steeple was added to the church in 1839 by R.D. Chantrell, the church itself was built in 1721 by William Etty.

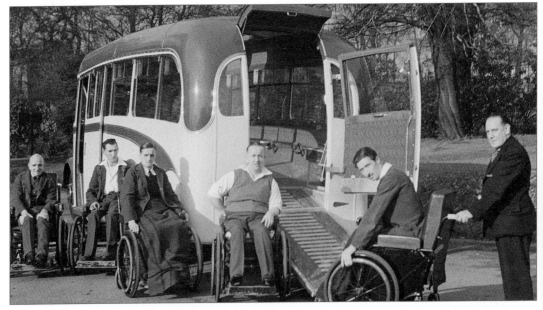

1949 A motor coach for disabled soldiers was provided by the City of Leeds Wounded Warriors' Welfare Committee, at the Ministry of Pensions Hospital, Chapel Allerton. The coach, built by Wilks & Mead Ltd of Leeds, was believed to be the first of its kind designed to convey wheelchair patients securely.

1950   A slum house cellar with boy, suggesting that he is having his weekly bath in a tin tub in front of the non-existent fire. There would no doubt have been some soap and water normally. Such conditions still existed in thousands of houses in the city, and demanded a major investment in slum clearance and improvement grants.

1950   Another common type of scullery in a slum dwelling with set pot for boiling clothes, gas ring for cooking and shallow stone sink.

1950 Benjamin Britten, the greatest British composer of the century, rehearsing his *Spring Symphony*, written the previous year, with the Hallé Orchestra for the Leeds Music Festival on 2 October. The festival was founded in 1858 and has been held in the Victoria Hall, Leeds Town Hall, ever since despite numerous postwar appeals for improved concert facilities.

1952 Lewis's in the Headrow (now Allders), with Harrison's almshouses in the background, the site of the St John's Centre. This photograph was taken on 23 August and shows the foundations for Headrow Buildings being excavated. The creation of an architectural unity along the north of the Headrow, according to plans produced by Sir Reginald Blomfield, took almost 30 years to realise.

1952   The main concourse of Leeds City station. Originally built in 1937 as the north concourse and hidden since the changes in 1967, it was restored to its former glory in early 1999 by Railtrack in a £165 million expansion programme.

1953   City Square and Queens Hotel as decorated in celebration of the coronation of Queen Elizabeth II on 2 June. Special 'See Your City' bus tours were run at 4*d* a time for a 25-mile tour to include the coronation decorations. One street, Oatland Terrace, Little London, was painted red, white and blue by its inhabitants.

79

1951   The Thoresby Society's 202nd excursion to Bolton Priory. Members gathered in the garden of the Ilkley home of the President, Professor John Le Patourel and Mrs Le Patourel. The Thoresby Society, the Leeds Local History Society, was founded in 1889. Based at Claremont, 23 Clarendon Road, where its library is housed, the society offers an annual publication and a course of winter lectures and summer excursions. A photograph by Harold G. Grainger FRPS.

1955   A flower show and fête at Cardigan House, a probation hostel of the Police Court Mission of the Diocese of Ripon. From the left is Col F. Eric Tetley (Chairman of Joshua Tetley & Son), Leonard W.L. Underwood, Arthur Schofield, Marion, Countess of Harewood, the opener, and Mrs Leonora Cohen. The latter became notorious as a suffragette, for smashing a display case of the Crown Jewels in the Tower of London in 1911. She was imprisoned in Armley Gaol. She then became the first woman president of the Leeds Trades Council in 1923, and a magistrate. She was to live to 105 years of age.

1951 Schofields' Golden Jubilee celebrations included a week of fashion offers entitled 'Fashion on a limited income'. The winner, on 11 May, was Mrs Gwen Wilkinson of Garforth, the centre of attention here. She won a complete ensemble styled for her by Erik, a London dress designer. She said she felt like 'Eliza Doolittle transformed into a duchess'.

1955 Allerton Grange Secondary Modern School on 22 April. A view of the library of the new 600-place county secondary school opened this year as a result of the rising birth rate in the immediate postwar period. All children were to continue their education to at least the age of fifteen.

1955 Weetwood Hall, University of Leeds Hall of Residence, with students strolling in the gardens on 25 May. In the 1955–6 academic year there were 3,551 full-time students. The idyllic location was not enough to encourage students to live so far from the university and the building has now been transformed into a major conference facility.

1956 Brotherton House under construction on 10 May. This seven-storey block of offices was built for £350,000 as the headquarters of Brotherton & Co. Ltd, chemical manufacturers. This company had been founded by Lord Brotherton of Roundhay Hall. The building was opened in January 1957. In April 1965, the building became the headquarters of Leeds City Police.

1957 Woodland Dye Works, demolished in the 1970s, on the footpath from Woodhouse Ridge to Grove Lane. A photograph by Stanley Robinson on 11 August.

1957 The Leeds Dam with the Saxton Gardens housing scheme under construction. The need for cheap but up-to-date housing was great as the war had restricted building materials to war-related construction. Slums at Marsh Lane were cleared and this complex of seven parallel slab blocks of flats was built five to ten storeys in height.

1957 River Aire from Leeds Bridge, with the Aire and Calder Navigation Warehouse on the right and warehouses on the Calls to the left. All the buildings in the picture have now been converted into apartments. In the background can be seen the tower of Leeds Parish Church. A photograph by Stanley Robinson on 7 September.

1958 HM the Queen's visit to Leeds on 17 October. Crowds lined the route from the station to the Civic Hall for the queen's tour of the city centre by car. Peacock & Son Ltd, soft furnishing store, cleared their shop windows on the Headrow to provide their customers and staff with a good view of proceedings.

1958 HM the Queen with Charles Henry Crabtree, Chairman and Managing Director of Crabtree & Sons Ltd, engineers and printing press manufacturers. He started work on the same day as the business was founded, on 6 May 1895. To that day he had worked for a total of 63 years for the company. The picture includes an impressive display of the many world newspapers printed on Crabtree presses. The company was taken over by Vickers in 1965 and relocated.

1959 The last Leeds tram, Horsfield no. 178, entered the Swinegate depot on 7 November at 7.30 p.m. Coins were being placed on the rails to be flattened under the wheels as a memento of the end of 88 years of tramway operation. With the death of the tram and the change to diesel-driven buses the Lord Mayor, Alderman Mrs G.A. Stevenson, questioned whether in 25 years time the bus would give way to the helicopter! That terrifying prospect was not fulfilled. But few imagined at that time that trams might return as the ultimate in efficient city transport.

1959 Hugh Gaitskell, MP for South Leeds since 1955, and leader of the Labour Party, watched the election results in a small room behind the platform at Leeds Town Hall, on the night of 8 October. This was the moment of defeat. Harold Macmillan's Conservative government was returned with an overall majority of 100 seats for an unprecedented third term. He was able to claim that the 'class war was obsolete'. At 1 a.m. on 9 October, with many more votes to come in, Gaitskell conceded victory.

Motorway City
of the '70s

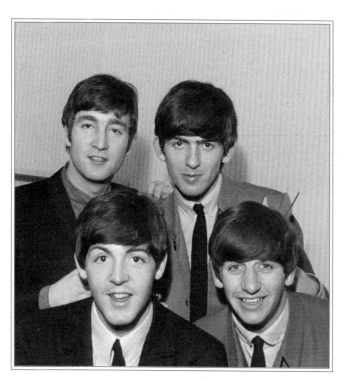

1963   The Beatles, who epitomised the 1960s for a generation. Here John Lennon, George Harrison, Paul McCartney and Ringo Starr are backstage, in the dressing room of the Odeon in the Headrow, on their second visit on 3 November. They played to a capacity audience of 2,500. Outside, 8,000 fans waited for a sight of the group. They had played the Odeon on 5 June, and came back again on 22 October 1964.

***c*. 1964** British Railways Neville Hill workshop with a 4–6–2 locomotive under maintenance. This atmospheric picture was taken by keen amateur photographer, Arthur Goldthorpe, of Horsforth Amateur Photographic Society.

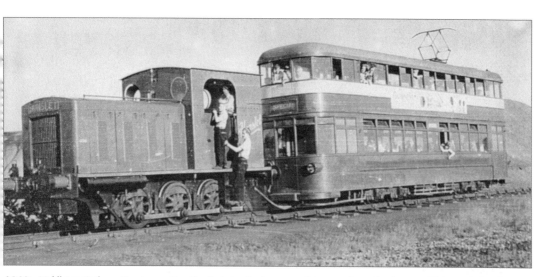

1960 Middleton Railway Trust operating the first standard gauge railway run by enthusiasts on 20 June. A diesel 0–6–0 No. 1697 built in 1934 by the Hunslet Engine Company was loaned by, and later purchased from the company. It was joined with a passenger-carrying double-decker railcar from the Swansea & Mumbles Railway. The railway that saw the first commercially successful steam locomotives, made by Matthew Murray, replace horsepower in 1812, now operates a regular passenger service.

1960 Norman Watson, Chairman and Managing Director of John Waddington Ltd at his desk in the Wakefield Road factory, continuing the family tradition of leading the company. The factory was demolished in the 1990s to make way for First Direct, the telephone banking service. Monopoly still holds pride of place on his desk, but the company was expanding into many other areas.

1962 Stanley Robinson, postal worker and keen amateur photographer, must have been a familiar sight at weekends taking photographs on his walks around the city. This amusing self-portrait was taken on 24 June somewhere in the city centre.

1962 Hough End Tannery of S. Gibson & Sons Ltd in Bramley was one of many tanneries in Leeds. The firm tanned goatskins into glazed kid for shoe making. Leeds was a national centre of this vital trade. The Tannery stood in the way of the Stanningley bypass scheme and was demolished in the late 1960s.

1962 Skilled operatives, at Hough End Tannery, who shaved leather in a traditional manner after the skins had been through numerous processes. These included being pasted on the flesh side with a paste of lime sulphide and arsenic.

1964 Mrs G.M. Peacock, senior family member of the board of directors of Peacock & Son, opening the newly refurbished store at the junction of Park Row and the Headrow. It marked the 115th anniversary of the foundation of the business. The store closed in 1977 but the business continued to operate from Kirkstall Bridge Mills until it was taken over by Durastic Ltd in 1981.

1965 A new parking meter. The city council brought in new measures to deal with traffic problems in the city centre, and parking meters were introduced to Leeds on 5 April. This photograph was taken by Stanley Robinson on 11 April.

1966 Sheepscar Branch Library. Along with the adjoining Chapeltown Post Office (now the Ramgharia Sikh Centre), the building survived in the Sheepscar clearance area. Partly occupied by the archives section of the Leeds Library Service in 1964, it is now the Leeds District Office of the West Yorkshire Archive Service. The service, part of West Yorkshire Joint Services, provides secure storage for the historical records of the metropolitan district. It accepts deposits from individuals and organisations that have significance for the history of the area. There is also a public searchroom for their consultation, by appointment.

1968 Bischoff House, otherwise called Sheepscar Hall, in North Street was owned by Nathaniel Denison in 1725. The impressive building sadly stood in the path of the new Inner Ring Road. It was demolished soon after this photograph was taken. In the background can be seen the new face of Leeds. On the left, the £6 million development of the Merrion Centre shopping and office complex opened in 1964 and the high-rise office block, Tower House, is under construction.

1968 Waterloo Main Colliery, Temple Pit, the last coal mine in Leeds to the south of Temple Newsam Park, closed around this time. The National Coal Board developed new plans in the 1970s for the opencasting of the site, known as 'the Shroggs'. This was estimated to produce a yield of 750,000 tons of coal with the ultimate objective of restoring the environment to attractive parkland.

1968 Leeds Civic Trust members at an Olde English social evening in Kirkstall Museum. The event was a great success and heavily oversubscribed, and 250 members and guests attended. The trust was established in 1965. Its aim was to stem the tide of destruction of the city's historic buildings, and promote high quality architectural design and town planning in the city, plus the improvement of public amenities.

1966 The first stage of the inner ring road, which laid waste the outskirts of the town centre between Westgate and Claypit Lane. Built to motorway standard it was designed as a principal traffic route around the city centre. The estimated cost was £2,144,081. In the picture taken on 11 July is Woodhouse Lane with the BBC studios to the left and Harewood Barracks, in the foreground, soon to be demolished to make way for new buildings for Leeds Central Colleges (by 1970 Polytechnic and after 1987 Leeds Metropolitan University).

1967 The general public enjoying the one and only opportunity to walk through the 1,200 ft tunnel section, since pedestrians and cyclists were to be prohibited from making use of the road once it was open. Ten thousand people were estimated to have made the effort before the official opening by the Lord Mayor, Alderman J.S. Walsh, on 14 January. (*Yorkshire Post*)

1967 Visit of the Minister of Transport, Barbara Castle MP, to the first stage of the inner ring road development. With her are Geoffrey Thirlwell, Leeds City Engineer, the Lord Mayor, Alderman J.S. Walsh and William Mackenzie Shand, representing the contractors.

1972 Billy Bremner, the Leeds United team captain, holding up the FA Cup after winning the Cup Final. Leeds United, managed by the legendary Don Revie, beat Arsenal by one goal. Bremner was United's most successful captain, winning two League championships, one FA cup, two Inter-Cities Fairs Cups, one League Cup and the Charity Shield. He is commemorated by a 9 ft bronze sculpture by Frances Segelman, unveiled at Elland Road by the club chairman, Peter Ridsdale, and Bremner's widow, Vicky, on 9 August 1999.

1971 The *Yorkshire Post* building on the corner of Bond Street and Albion Street before it moved to new premises in Wellington Road on the site of the former Bean Ing Woollen Factory, the oldest of its kind in the world. Founded as the *Leeds Intelligencer* in 1754, the newspaper had added the name *Yorkshire Post* in 1866 and then simplified the title in 1883.

1971 Children playing in the street near Servia Hill, Woodhouse, as the process of slum clearance drew to a close. Large-scale objection brought a change of policy to one of improvement rather than demolition.

1971 Marshall & Snelgrove's department store holding a closing down sale. It formed part of the Debenham's chain which included the nearby Matthias Robinson store. The latter store was to be upgraded at a cost of £250,000. A spokesman observed that 'younger people tended not to buy volumes of high priced fashions but more of less expensive items'. Forty years earlier it had been the place to be seen: 'anyone who was anyone in the county met in the restaurant for two hour lunches', it was said.

1971 Leeds Civic Trust Pedestrian Precinct Standing Committee in Lands Lane. The scheme included the three trees planted to soften the urban landscape and convert this part of Leeds into an oasis for shoppers. The Chairman of the Trust, John Hepper, stands to the right of the tree with Sir Frank Marshall, leader of Leeds City Council, to the left. The committee commissioned a competitive design for a water feature in the lower portion of Lands Lane. None of these features has survived the pace of change in the city centre.

1975 Geoffrey Boycott, Herbert Sutcliffe and Len Hutton. A historic picture of three century-makers for Yorkshire together on 17 June at Headingley Cricket Ground.

1975 Ian Chappell, the Australian team captain, and Tony Greig, the England team captain, inspected the pitch at Headingley on 19 August. The wicket was damaged by supporters of George Davis, a London taxi driver, sentenced to 20 years for taking part in an armed robbery in which a policeman was shot. England had set the Australians 445 to win in the third test but the match had to be abandoned. England's chances of regaining the Ashes were doomed.

1975 Kirkgate Market was destroyed on the night of 13 December by the worst fire in the city's history. Caused by an electrical fault, two-thirds of the building, over 4 acres, was razed to the ground. It took over 100 firemen, using 15 pumps and 31 water jets, to combat the blaze. Damage was estimated at £7 million but there were no casualties. It was in Kirkgate Market that the Marks & Spencer empire began with one stall.

1976 The interior of the restored covered Leeds market was completed by 19 July, as a temporary measure, to enable traders to get back into business. A major restoration programme was under way by 1991. A more ambitious scheme was abandoned after two public enquiries. Kirkgate Market is now one of the largest markets in Europe with over 500 tenants, attracting over 100,000 shoppers on a single Saturday.

1978 Victor Watson, dynamic Chairman of John Waddington Ltd, was the third generation of the family to head the company. He promoted the successful line of *Star Wars* puzzles at the Birmingham Games and Toys Fair with a storm trooper and R2D2. The product manager at the time predicted that *Star Wars* would 'within a few years . . . . probably be forgotten as a film'. The games side of the company was sold to Hasbro in 1994.

1978 The Duke of Edinburgh attended the 9th meeting of his Award Scheme in Leeds Civic Hall on 26 October with the Lord Mayor, Councillor Harry Booth. He later visited a display of award scheme activities at the College of Building.

1978 Intrigued bystanders watched a Keep Fit demonstration in the square in front of the Central Library in the Headrow on 12 July. A hundred office workers and shoppers turned out for a session organised by a firm of toiletry manufacturers. It provided a great deal of harmless amusement for the general public, and an opportunity for the acute eye of newspaper photographer, John Varley.

1979 The Rt Hon. Dennis Healey, MP and Chancellor of the Exchequer, with his wife Edna. They were about to set off to canvass in his constituency of East Leeds on the last day of the election campaign on 3 May. At the election the Conservatives won 339 seats to Labour's 268.

103

1976   The Yorkshire Water float in the parade to celebrate the 350th anniversary of the receipt of the first charter by the city. Ninety floats took part in this the third Lord Mayor's Parade on 26 June.

1976   Members of the Sealed Knot Society in the parade add a little authentic period colour.

The Fastest Growing
City in Britain

1987 Princess Anne visited Beeston, in February, as President of the Save the Children Fund. She wore a fur hat and classic camel coat. She received the traditional Bangladeshi floral garland of welcome made up of chrysanthemums and carnations, at the Asha Neighbourhood Unit. The unit assisted immigrant families to settle into the English way of life.

1982   HM the Queen accompanied by Henry Moore left the City Art Gallery, after opening the new extension and Henry Moore Sculpture Centre. She admired his sculpture '*Reclining Woman (Elbow) 1980*' that has pride of place on the forecourt.

1982   Gatecrashers at the Rolling Stones' concert in Roundhay Park, 25 July. The first major open-air rock concert to be staged at the park was a sell-out – 90,000 tickets were sold, but police and organisers estimated that a further 20,000 people climbed in over the fence. The venue has since attracted other leading artists like Bruce Springsteen in 1984, and Michael Jackson in 1988.

1982 The Prince and Princess of Wales leaving St Gemma's Hospice, Moortown, on 30 March. They opened the £2 million extension to the building which had become a hospice in 1978. She wore an emerald green maternity coat and matching hat and revealed that the baby (the future Prince William) was expected to be born on 1 July.

1982 The West Indian Carnival about to set off with the queen, Valerie Daley, and the designer and organiser, Arthur France. The first such carnival was held in Chapeltown on August Bank Holiday 1967. It then attracted 5,000 people and has since seen increasing crowds every year. Its success sent a message to other Caribbean communities, and the London Notting Hill event followed in 1968. Arthur France was the inspiration behind the carnival in Leeds which he had dreamed of ever since arriving from Nevis in 1957. He set up the United Caribbean Association in 1964, with George Archibald and Cedric Clarke, and formed a Carnival Organising Committee to fund-raise. He was awarded the MBE for his efforts for the community.

1986 Cockburn High School, Burton Road, Hunslet. One of two Higher Grade schools built by the Leeds School Board before it was legally entitled to do so. Famous for the education of former pupils like Richard Hoggart, Willis Hall and Sir Ernest Woodroofe it had to be demolished. It was found to be full of asbestos and could not easily be adapted to modern teaching requirements. New premises were built nearby.

1986 Fletland Mills building on the River Aire on 26 September. An historic building on the River Aire, dating from the late eighteenth century and ripe for redevelopment. In 1992 the derelict structure was turned into the 4-star award-winning hotel 42 The Calls, as part of the revival of the whole area into a thriving mix of apartments, office blocks and hotels.

1986 Jimmy Savile arriving hot-foot for his honorary doctorate award at the University of Leeds. Today the most famous personality in the city, and one who has remained a committed 'Loiner'. Not only has he become a household name as a television performer, but he has quietly given generously of his time by regularly helping patients at Leeds General Infirmary and other hospitals.

1986 Oulton Hall, Rothwell, was a sad shell of a building. Formerly the home of the Calverley family, major landowners in the Rothwell area, it had grounds landscaped by Humphrey Repton. The building had been intended for a police headquarters. This did not happen and the hall was carefully redeveloped by De Vere hotels into a prestigious new facility, with an adjoining golf course.

1986 The Grand Theatre, New Briggate, is the home of the highly regarded Opera North company, which was formed in 1978. The theatre itself was purchased by the city council in 1973 and provides a venue for a range of other productions including pre-West End tours.

1987 Edwina Currie, controversial Minister of Health, at Killingbeck Hospital to see the special cardiac unit for children. Within ten years the hospital was demolished and the facilities moved to new premises at Leeds General Infirmary.

1988 Armley Mills Industrial Museum. The city council purchased the mill building in 1969 for a new museum celebrating Leeds' industrial past. The building dates from 1805 but a mill has operated on the site for over 400 years.

1990   River Aire at Granary Wharf. This area at the junction of the River Aire and the Leeds and Liverpool Canal has been turned into a visitor attraction with specialist shops and craft fairs. Barge trips are run on the waterways. In the background is the Asda headquarters, built in 1988. This building was the catalyst for further development of the run-down riverside.

1990   Alan Bennett, novelist and playwright, and Barbara Taylor Bradford, novelist, were both born in Leeds. They each received the honorary award of Doctor of Letters on 11 May at the University of Leeds.

1990 The Victoria Quarter. This major refurbishment of Queen Victoria Street, County and Cross Arcades by the Prudential, costing some £6 million, has created a unique shopping environment and brought together a mix of leading and independent retailers. In 1996 it enticed Harvey Nichols, upmarket Knightsbridge store, to locate its first development outside London here.

1992 The St Valentine's Fair in the city centre. The city council is keen to encourage families back into the city centre with events like this.

1992 Civic Reception for Leeds United after winning the League Championship. Gordon Strachan, the team captain, holds the cup for the crowd. Under their manager, Howard Wilkinson, Leeds once again tasted success. An estimated crowd of 150,000 people thronged the streets on Sunday 3 May, to pay homage to the team.

1997 Thackray Medical Museum opened in part of St James' Hospital, formerly the Beckett Street workhouse, on 25 March. The museum illustrates in gruesome detail the impact that medicine has made on our lives. The core of the museum is the collection assembled by Paul Thackray of the firm of Charles F Thackray, surgical instrument makers of Leeds.

1997 View of City Square with new buildings to the north in October. Two major rebuildings have enhanced the appearance of the square. The Norwich Union Insurance Company employed architects Abbey Hanson Rowe to rebuild No. 1 City Square and NatWest Properties has commissioned Fletcher Joseph Partnership to renew No. 1 Park Row. They are the third buildings on these prime sites in this century.

1997 West Yorkshire Archaeological Service excavating a Roman road within yards of the new M1/A1 link road at Aberford. This road ran between Castleford and Tadcaster. Before its destruction by the new Hook Moor Interchange there was time to discover that the road was constructed on an *agger* or bank of interleaved layers of sub-soil and limestone, about 6 metres wide and over 1 metre in height. On top of the *agger* there was a metalled road surface. This service is a member of the West Yorkshire Joint Services together with Archives. Grants and Trading Standards.

1999   The Epicentre at Meanwood Valley Urban Farm, an interpretation and visitors' centre for the farm based on sustainable technology. Built by trainees with the aid of a Millennium Lottery Fund grant this project is an educational facility aimed to encourage visitors to learn how they can make a difference in reducing their use of the earth's natural resources.

1998   Bankside School, winners of the Stan Kenyon Annual Schools Challenge Competition 'Rubbish Ideas' with the Lord Mayor, Councillor Mrs Linda Middleton. This competition established by the former City Planning Chief encourages schoolchildren to think about today's environmental issues.

1997   The opening day of a specially designed skateboard and rollerblade park on Woodhouse Moor on 4 October. It has provided welcome facilities for local youth in the summer months.

1998   Clare Higgins as Liz, Ian McKellen as Garry Essendine and Susie Baxter as Monica Reed in *Present Laughter* by Noel Coward at the West Yorkshire Playhouse, Quarry Hill. The play was part of a continuing programme that has made the Playhouse, in the words of *The Independent* in 1998, 'a major powerhouse for the North in the nineties'. Photograph by Keith Pattison.

1999 Centenary Bridge and Tetley's Brewery Wharf. The £6 million development of the Brewery Wharf houses an interpretation centre that celebrates the colourful story of the British pub. So that it could be easily accessible from the city centre it was necessary to build a new bridge across the River Aire in 1993. This was called the Centenary Bridge to commemorate the centenary of the grant of city status to Leeds.

1999 Lands Lane with continental-style café. The encouragement of the city council has brought people back into the city centre. Pedestrianisation has kept traffic out of some streets. The Leeds City Centre Initiative, working with local businesses, has created more leisure opportunities. The city looks increasingly like a European city.

1999 Royal Armouries Museum tiltyard, with the restored 1824 flax mill, Rose Wharf, in the background. This innovative attraction is only one of many that has made the £42.5 million purpose-built museum a must for visitors to the city. Built on a 13-acre site on Clarence Dock only ten minutes walk from the city centre, the museum's purpose is to explore the impact that arms and armour have had on the development of mankind. Formerly at the Tower of London the collection housed here is one of the world's greatest. It was opened in March 1996 by HM the Queen.

1999 Leeds and Bradford Airport check-in desk for departure. Established in 1931 as a municipal aerodrome on 60 acres of grassland, it began scheduled flights in 1935 to Newcastle, Edinburgh, Blackpool and the Isle of Man. Since 1987 it has been run as a limited company with the five Metropolitan District Councils of West Yorkshire as shareholders. The main runway was extended in the same year so that it could accommodate Boeing 747 jumbo jets. When Concorde flew from the airport for the first time 70,000 people came to watch. This year some 1.4 million passengers have used the airport.

1996 The statue of Edward, the Black Prince, by Thomas Brock was completed in 1903 and erected as the centrepiece of City Square. The figure was chosen by the benefactor, Alderman T. Walter Harding, to symbolise chivalry, good government, patronage of the arts and education, encouragement of industry, and democratic values. It is fitting to end the century by reference to this surviving commemoration of the newly created city of 1893. The equestrian statue still awaits the creation of a suitably grand piazza and points proudly and optimistically towards Europe.

Acknowledgements and Picture Credits

In the short time available for completing this volume it is surprising the debt that one runs up to so many people who have rallied round to help one out. By the most amazing good fortune I was enabled to check through most of Leeds Central Library's photographic collection just before its removal to storage and make a selection of images. For this facility I am most grateful to Michele Lefevre and her colleagues in the Family and Local History Library. David Sheard has done an immaculate job of preparing quality black and white prints from not always perfect originals and in a very short time. Thanks are due to the Lord Mayor's office staff, Geoff Jones, Mick Roo, Ian Stafford and Martin Searle and their colleagues in Leeds Planning Department, Graphics Agency. Mary Forster, Hon. Librarian of the Thoresby Society, was extremely helpful in providing a selection of images. I must also acknowledge the ready assistance of Dr Mark Shipway, Archivist, Leeds University Archives, Dr Kevin Grady, Director, Leeds Civic Trust, Dr Max Farrar, Leeds Metropolitan University, Sarah Scott, West Yorkshire Playhouse, Sheila Bye, Middleton Railway Trust, Mike Fisher, the *Yorkshire Post*, Victor Watson and Richard Peacock. John Varley has been very generous with prints from his own collection as has Arthur Goldthorpe. Mark Shelton and Peter Eveleigh have also provided vital information.

I am conscious of the forbearance and good will of my colleagues, Bill Connor, Alexandra Eveleigh, Gladys Lindley and Alan Carter and most grateful to them for assisting in the whole process and to Lisa Watson for standing in for a month at short notice. My wife Felicity has been, as ever, a stalwart support even when, at the same time, under the pressure of her own projects.

West Yorkshire Archive Service: Leeds, pp: half-title page, 2, 3, 6, 8, 16, 17, 19, 20, 21, 24, 25, 26, 27, 29 (bottom), 31, 32, 35, 36, 37, 41, 42, 44 (top), 45, 46 (top), 48, 49, 50 (bottom), 51, 53 (bottom), 54 (bottom), 55, 56, 57, 58, 60, 61, 63, 64 (top), 65, 66 (bottom), 67, 68, 73, 75, 76, 80 (bottom), 81, 82 (top), 83, 84, 85, 87, 88, 89, 90, 91, 92, 93, 94 (top), 95 (top), 96, 98; Leeds City Libraries front endpaper, 22, 29 (top), 30, 33, 34, 38, 39, 40, 43, 44 (bottom), 47 (top), 52 (bottom), 53 (top), 54 (top), 66 (top), 69, 70, 71, 72, 74, 77, 78, 79, 82 (bottom); Thoresby Society, 18, 46 (bottom), 50 (top), 52 (top), 62, 80 (top); Leeds University, 23; Victor Watson, 28; *Yorkshire Post*, 64 (bottom), 95 (bottom); John Varley, 86 (bottom), 97, 100, 101, 105, 106, 109, 111 (top), 112 (bottom); Leeds Civic Trust, 94 (bottom), 99; Max Farrar,107 (bottom); Leeds City Planning, 108 (top), 111 (bottom), 113, 114 (top), 115 (top), 116, 117 (top), 118 (bottom), 120, back endpaper; Leeds City Council, Lord Mayor's Office, 6; West Yorkshire Playhouse [Keith Pattison], 117 (bottom); Felicity Harrison, 118 (top), 119.

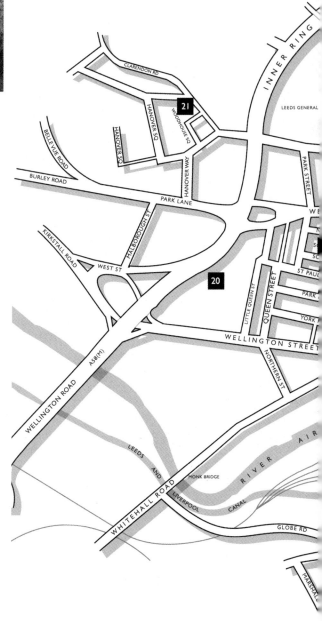

City Centre Leisure and Shopping.

1. Merrion Centre
2. Bond Street Centre
3. St. Johns Centre
4. Schofields Centre
5. Kirkgate Market
6. Corn Exchange
7. Crown Point Retail Park
8. Harvey Nichols
9. Royal Armouries
10. Tetleys Brewery Wharf
11. Gateway Yorkshire
12. Parish Church
13. West Yorkshire Playhouse
14. City Bus Station
15. Grand Theatre
16. Dark Arches / Granary Wharf
17. Leeds Central Library (reopening 2000)
18. Art Gallery and Henry Moore
    Foundation
19. Park Square
20. International Pool
21. Yorkshire Archaeological
    Society/Thoresby Society
22. West Yorkshire Archive Service: Leeds
23. Millennium Square (completion 2000)

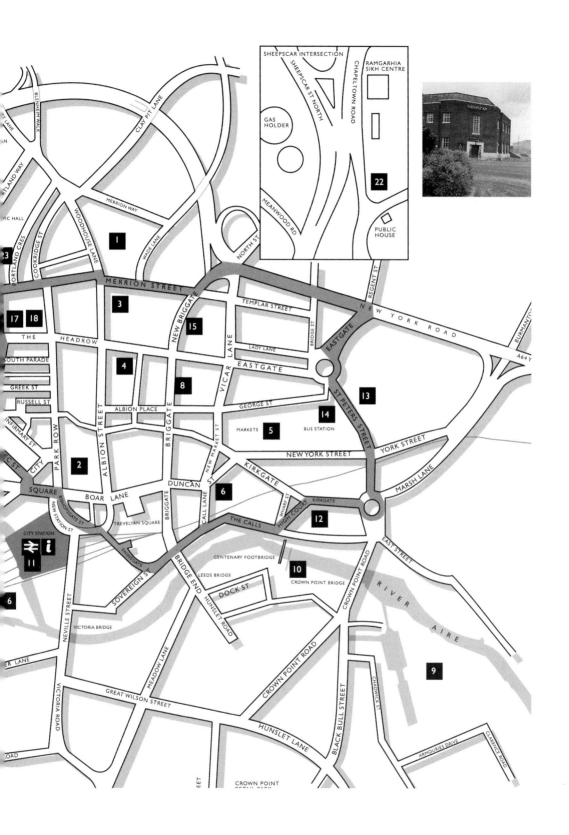